You Know Who You Are

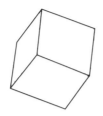

YOU KNOW WHO YOU ARE

IAN WILLIAMS

Wolsak & Wynn

Cover image: Irina Souiki
Cover Design and Layout: Jared Roberts
Typeset in Plantin
Printed by Coach House Books Toronto, Canada

The publisher gratefully acknowledges the support of the Canada Council
for the Arts, the Ontario Arts Council and the Canada Book Fund for
their financial assistance.

Wolsak and Wynn Publishers Ltd.
#102–69 Hughson Street North
Hamilton, ON
Canada L8R 1G5

Library and Archives Canada Cataloguing in Publication

Williams, Ian, 1979-
You Know Who You Are / Ian Williams.

Poems.

ISBN 978-1-894987-41-7

I. Title.

PS8645.I562Y68 2010   C811'.6   C2010-900118-4

for four Js

*who know who
they are*

Contents

Look at You

Emergency Codes

I MEAN I

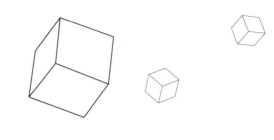

You can't go thinking you are better than other people just because you can learn poems. Who do you think you are?

– Alice Munro, *Who Do You Think You Are?*

When suddenly she realized…words were –…what? …who? … no! … she!

– Samuel Beckett, *Not I*

It is not as if an "I" exists independently over here and then simply loses a "you" over there, especially if the attachment to "you" is part of what composes who "I" am. If I lose you, under these conditions, then I not only mourn the loss, but I become inscrutable to myself. Who "am" I, without you?

– Judith Butler, *Precarious Life*

But I am a worm, and no man.

– Psalm 22:6

"ANYBODY COULD LOVE YOU? LOOK AT YOU. LOOK AT YOUR FACE."

Don't ask. She (don't ask) did not say it
to me. She did not mean it now. Please don't
make anything of– She said it to my–
and all right she meant it then. Leave it alone.
That I remember it at all – all droopy, soaked through
with chromatics – blame the drizzle, the night,
the red-eye flight, the slow WiFi. *Anybody could love you?*
Really. Enough.

Looks like static in the lamplight, the rain,
interferes with. Then – sudden – the whole sky's up
in my eye, a watch face bouncing light. Look. *Look at you.*
Look here, I said stop. *Look at your face.*

Now you understand
why I got back to you so late. I ignored the call for days,
the voicemail icon at the top of the display,
ignored the options *Listen Dismiss*, the area code,
the last four digits I miss. And why, when I finally could, I couldn't
listen to the last part *Anybody could love you* of your message,
look at you the part you whispered *look at your face* without hearing
something like a newspaper shake.
You could be anybody.

LOOK AT YOU

Not saying

Fists in our sleeves, we reach our limit. No way
past Lake Ontario, nothing else to do
until you say the thing you need to say.

Sweeten it if you like. Stir in a name.
It's only talk and we've talked our heads to
foam before, testing the limit in a way.

Like the last time our four feet inched partway
over the city's ledge. Lightheaded you
started to say something you needed to say

then started again, *We could – we can fly one way.*
Right over the lake. How you said it, as if we were two
wild geese, no credit limit in the way. Ain't no way,

I said. *Way.* No way. *Way.* Tonight at the lake
your courage fails again. Knuckles in your pits, you
flap your arms and squawk. Say what you're dying to say.

Of course, don't. We're getting carried away.
We'll stay this side of Lake Ontario, clenched. *Nous*
sommes à la limite de l'amitié – find a way
to translate. If you won't say, I won't say.

the sky's disapproval
you rode 20 km along the Don Valley Parkway to tell me
in person *I've decided to make myself into a machine.*
That explains the reflective garb, stiff hair and sunglasses.
You're on a mission

*to return to the present and prevent
the future.* Your Terminator eye reddens. Or *protect it.* I forget.
In the lightning you're mercurial. And *the future?* A plane to Boston
at 300 km/month. By my count, we have many goodbyes to go
before I go.

A machine I say, about to straddle my bike. *Hurrah.*
Let me know how Then I notice how *that works for you* our two bikes
nestle antlers. Their turned-in wheels, two lowered heads,
nuzzle.

You crouch to eye level, release the chain
and stroke the rough skin of the tire as if it were your own kind.
I cannot leave now without treading mud across your hand
or your neck.

Say it like Ah-nold and I'll let you go.
20 km in the rain for a promise. *I'll be back.* But by then you'll be
all derailleur, suspension, odometer, all metal, rubber, black
grease and air. Satisfied you throw your head back to fuel,
just your throat moves

                                   just your throat moves
as you drink back everything left to say. The screws holding us
in place slacken. I will leave now and months from now
I will become undetectable, suspicious, an alarming blip
in your eye's sweeping circular radar.

Poor reception, so you say
you have to lean out a window to *Hello? Hello?*
call, mouth jammed with static, with scorched grass
Hello? That you? and just before you cut out, I call you back,
Quaker-like, *my friend.*

Good call. I made a mistake. This is not friendship.

I have a name, you remind me. You are not my anything.
Certainly not some youknowwho *Hello? Can you hear me?*
the kind of woman who sleeps on her side, curlers in,
and wonders *What went wrong? What happened to pookie?*

Careful now, don't be calling no one *pookie.*

Hello? Hello? Main menu. Press 1 if you want
me to go somewhere. *Hell*– Press 2 if you want me
to listen *Hello?* to thee, my friend, to thee. Press 3
for more options. 0 if you want me to speak.

Let's not kid ourselves. This is not friendship.
This is a service.
When you call you
will get what you want. Not me. The machine.

MISUNDERSTANDINGS

Walking you tell me you dreamt
you were flying for the first time.

You smile down at your feet
as they sink through the snow

but it's the same dream my friend,
you've described it before, only

you've changed *falling to flying*. Remember
the morning you woke in a bathtub

of ball bearings, dropped by a man
and with both legs broken?

crying *why?*

why me? why why? melodramatically
rattling your fists in the air.

It rained all day the day your body came
dismantled in the tub. *My tears,* you said

in that Bollywood way you have.
The rain will never end, never never end.

And alas today it is snowing– you
are snowing, you'd have me believe

the whites of your eyes cracked red
between your lashes, your lids sinking.

Not your legs but your heart
broken that day in the bathtub

and now it flutters so well you dream
you're flying. My friend (*would you stop*

calling me that?) it means you're better,
better than or better off or better off without.

My friend (*are you for real?*) – you want me
to call you more than my friend? After the falling,

the flying, all that crying, you've ended up
here we are walking calf-deep in snow.

MISTAKES

this is how
this is how people   make mistakes
      people like you make mistakes

this is how people make people
this is how people make   mistakes

this is how   people make
    people make   mistakes

this is how people make people ~~like you~~
this is how people like you make ~~people~~ mistakes

people like you make mistakes
    you make people like mistakes

    you like people how is this
        this is how people like you

people like you

~~you like people~~

people like you make
people like you

you make
        mistakes
                make you make
                        mistakes

WEST OF BOSTON

The streets tighten
from four lanes to two, buckle from graph paper
to spider veins. *Wherefore have ye brought us up*
out of Egypt to die in the wilderness? Those people,
always murmuring.
                              Sun warps the hills
are spoiled broccoli, autistic men tumble out a bus
to work the bakery no one buys from. No one works
the old mills, their eyes boxed shut. Sirens strobe
and gravel-kicking kids take off. It's all so
used to have and *used to be.*

Lo. A coffee shop opens, a dress code, jazz,
girls push their strollers into shady parks, and.
You think you're too good for us here. The radiator
conks out. Men cheer their teams. *You think we're*
beneath you. You have to shift to second to make it
up South St. Come now. The dark knees we wear,
the morning phlegm, the low-grade heart murmur
give up give up. It's all so. Might as well.

GIVE UP

black,
change, dye, *only $9.99*, talking too much
about – what? – the weekend, overhearing,

yes for a while,
then no, forgetting the names of people
you may never meet again, you might,

what for?

OPEN

To correctly open
a package of ramen – a college student showed me – hold it,
fly up, in both hands, and snap till your knuckles ram each other.
You will feel the bones inside – sardine spines – dislocate
before they break.

Didn't my Lord deliver Daniel
And the correct way to eat it – nobody has to tell me this –
deliver Daniel is not from the pot over the sink *deliver Daniel*
but as if someone boiled it for you *Didn't my Lord deliver Daniel*
that's before alimony, before the rumpled face *and why not*
every man al dente and after grace.

Except you

                    don't say– we don't
say things like _____ round here.

Even with the mute of square states, time zones,
weather between us, we still won't. We tip
the phone from our ear, fill our mouths
with sponge: *Have a good night* or *That's it
for me* and hang up quickly, just in case
one of us doesn't say it or does.
A hum in our throats, a trill, a clearing:
I love you and *don't say it.*

                    Once my grandmother
came close. I saw her throat, her hands, warble.
My grandfather had just come home from the hills
in Speyside, noontime, hat still on from the sun,
and she said, *I'm glad you're back safely* – formal,
wiping her palms on the pleats of her dress.

When he died the villagers were afraid
she would wander into the hills with his rusty cutlass
and pheasants tied around his old belt, calling after him
in shrill falsetto. She never wandered. Or they found her
before she did. She never called him anything
except *you.*

TRIOLET FOR *YOU*

There is no synonym for *you.*
A billion names for men like me
and none for you. *None.* Not a few.
There is no synonym for *you.*
The thesaurus says, *No match. Do
you mean yogi?* May I use *thee?*
No, there is no synonym for you.
A billion names for men like me.

Special

You want proof that we are. You're sopped
in romance novel covers, doo-wop nostalgia, damn Shakespeare.
I tell you stories of men throwing themselves on grenades, arms
and legs spread as if to embrace, to save their men. We would
never do that, not for a chest full of metal, not even for each other.
But people do. People do. We have enough trouble

laying ourselves down, waiting to be launched or diffused. *So long
lives this and this gives life to thee.* Bunk. Don't believe it. *So long
as men can breathe and eyes can see* anyone with a wedding video,
an answering machine, anyone licking ice cream in the back blur
of an amusement park photo will outlive us. How's that for proof?

It's not what you want to hear. You want to know *who put the bomp
in the bomp bah bomp bah bomp?* and I go on about airplanes bursting
into orange feathers and how some people never die because they believe,
and how others have to satisfy themselves with something near
immortality: the first-period teacher who wheeled in the TV
that September. Bystanders open their palms to the residue
for the dust of spectacular deaths to freckle them. Here's your proof:
We lay hands on each other.
                    Nothing. Not even heat.

You say it

as if I had forgotten
as if words make something happen
and you say it as if your finger, not a receiver,
were under my chin, stroking *coochie coochie coo.*

You say it with the tightly shut eyes of a seven-year-old
in prayer, a tomboy who asks God for the latest
Teenage Mutant Ninja Turtle. And gets it. Asks God
for a friend. And gets me. Then, propped on her elbows,
face open on the sepal of her hands, she goes on
all winter evening make believing.
                                        You say it with all
the smugness of *I told you so* because I didn't at first believe
you could turn a book into a tent, a plastic bag
into the sewers, Barbie into Splinter, me into sidekick.
Because I said so, you explain.

                                        I blink as if coming
out of a dark theatre. *Let there be light.*

V

I

Vicarious

See how cold it is.
Trees tap the window and snap
back, burned by hot glass.

II

Vacillate

Where's the fire? Your ex
tinguisher's sputtering foam.
Let the forest burn. Just

delay a little. Go late.
Please stay but stay over there.

III

Virgin

What word will keep you?
need love yes sick also no
no no no no no

IV

Vandalize

Outside a man leans
on his shovel and watches
cars with white mohawks

brake. So much ice, punk snow ploughs
brake. Wires, branches break. You won't.

V

Visceral

Minor muscle sprains
and swollen parts call for ice.
Never heat the heart.

You know who you are

You're looking worse.
Overbitten, underkissed, bottom teeth a shambles
like an old beach house fence. Why you never smile.
You of the slack tricep. Slack elastic. Jockey drawer's
been white cotton for decades. Toilet bowl's stained,
seat's spattered with dried piss.
About as sexy
as herringbone or a preposition. Honourable
mention. Prufrock, Polonius, Millhouse. Just a friend.
A best friend. Just a friend.

Love handled. Juliet-sleeved mustard bridesmaid.
Alto in the church choir, can't remember the words
to *The Lord in Zion Reigneth*. Piano quitter. Median child. Fourth
or fifth pick for street hockey. In tag, it. Nursed on juice boxes
by Super Mario brothers, a key round your neck.

Today alone
missed the eight-glass water quota, missed five to ten
servings of whatever, did not floss, missed the ex, couldn't resist
sitcom after syndicated sitcom, *Law & Order*, then *Late*
and *Late Late Shows*, their cynical hosts looking at the audience
behind the cameras but not you, God too turning his head
in disgust – how long have you had
to work things out?

You're looking real bad these days.

I don't have anything else to say.
I don't have to say anything else.

EMERGENCY CODES

Emergency Codes

Is this anything that couldn't wait?
the police will say.

Too much bass never killed nobody.
You'll look like a yuppie fool yammering
bout my boy's music – he ain't no gangsta,
here ain't no ghetto. What you know
bout his girl? She sixteen, she pregnant. So?

Nobody broke in. That's the smoke alarm.
It's all smoke.

                      Is this any emergency –
a dirty burner, a blown bulb, a music video flashing
monsters on the wall?

CODE PINK: INFANT ABDUCTION

Don't be stupid. He wasn't born in jail.
The fights Dre brags about, throwing it down
in the yard, punishment in solitary, tallying
time on the wall – all that's from his time
at Spruce Lake K–8.

But before that he spent nine months locked up
in me. My friend was pregnant same time.
When her baby broke and opened its eyes
she clapped a hand to her chest. *Blue. They're blue.*
Like his father.

What of the fatherless?
I knew Dre's colour before he was born, knew everything
in fact – pricey sneakers, hoops and hoods, 2 a.m. clubs –
so when he opened his, I looked down on him
with my own black eyes unsurprised.
After all you only mine.

CODE PURPLE: CHILD ABDUCTION

Dre's teacher, a Mrs., thinks my boy's dirty
he's so dark because his neck lumps
into rings like a dark Michelin man

and his hair, cornrowed back
with petroleum jelly, doesn't change
patterns often enough. She best stick

to teaching and leave off hairdressing
and psychotherapy: *Would you prefer*
to sit quietly there or join us and sing?

and *We don't use words like that here* and
Inside voice finger to her lip. She wrong
to make him think he got a choice.

If this were a different place, Rwanda say,
he'd have a gun the length of her arm.
She might sponsor him for the cost of a cup

of coffee. If this were a different time,
she wouldn't bother with that nonsense.
Just whip him for no reason. Well

there's always a reason: for being
so black, so damn useless with his child hands.

Code White: Medical Emergency (Pediatric)

When Dre was about nine he and a friend
tried to pierce their ears with a thumbtack
and a stapler. Quick. Where Dr. Huxtable at?
Boys. I tell you.
                              Remember the time
Theo pierced his ear (*I'm a man*) and it got infected
and Dr. Huxtable found out and got his little black bag
to clean it up? It was like that
                              minus the black bag,
Dr. Huxtable, Theo, the live studio audience
laughter and applause.

                              It's time to blame someone.
Not Dre or his friend or the school system,
the government, sitcoms, hip hop videos,
the streets, whatever. I don't blame myself either.

That leaves you. Maybe I blame you a little.
Because. You. Should have.

Code Blue: Medical Emergency (Adult)

>   Folks like us, we
> don't get assassinated, we
> get shot.
>
> He dreams of it / many times / being shot
> in black and white like a classy gangsta film.
>
> I'm in the dream too, jumbo-sized,
> bawling after the gurney, bawling down
> the hospital corridor like a Doppler siren.
>
> The rest of the plot is what you'd see on TV:
> IVs thread him whole again
>   to exact revenge
> with a slow-motion frown and a semicircle
> of fire sparking from his gun.
>
>   That's what he wants –
> that and his name like an ice cube in everyone's cheek:
> *Did you see? Did you see how he iced that punk? how he–*
>
> *Respect*, he calls this smiling. *Nuff respect.*

CODE RED: FIRE

Fired. Past tense. My baby's
almost always fired

for something as simple as
deep tanning the fries, missing the bus, nothing
much. Sometimes for nothing. Dre's boss, sweating
a moustache, bearing a fat isosceles of skin
over his belt buckle, says *Look, we're downsizing.*
You knew this was coming.

Because I'm black, Dre tells me,
so he sits at home, picking at his face, picking
at his face, until he goes from black to white to raw.

Then he gets a telemarketing job. Assumes
everyone on the other side is white. Is he
wrong?

Code Yellow: Bomb Threat

Will he ever be the same again?
Day in, day out, he risks going out
of style.

Still here?

Hours after the sun bombs his bed
he jacks half up in the latest

thuggear, dusting his rubbled face
who's the bomb baby? already dressed
in clothes that disappear.

Still here?

And he spits a language that only grows (explosive) and grows (extinct)

Code Silver: Person with a Weapon

Didn't know bout the girl
till, you know, she got fat.

For her hunger he gave her
a dirty word to suck on –

one that started small then grew
from four letters to five. She answers

to both. Dre had shot so many
blanks, empty calories, stray

conjugations that I never thought
he could start his own cell

but he did, not alone, but he did
it.

CODE GREY: COMBATIVE PERSON

Not in my house, I said when he lost
his job again and took up hunting

weed. He'd come out of his room
swiping the joint skin gainst his tongue

with that firemouthed hoochie
in the background. I was blunt

with her. No choice. No ultimatum.
She said, *Ima do what I wanna do.*

Who you think you is? And she upped
and threw her pregnant self down the night

and cracked open with life and sense
and milk. And Dre, terrified, I flooded

with mother noise bout the glock
he'd like to keep under his ribs, not

a soul at the end of its bullet. *Let me
show you how to kill something,* I said,

besides time. He: *You workin me over.* Me:
I'm making you work.

CODE ORANGE: HAZARDOUS SPILL

A baby. The pressure. The press started shooting
immediately. In case. In this one you can still see
some blood on the li'l thing's face. Here's one
before they cleaned the vernix, his hair slick
with amniotic oil, styled like a duck
after an oil spill.

              Yeah, paparazzi up in our faces,
neighbours blathering – *grandmother's a heifer,*
girl's a hussy, boy's a gangsta, baby's a stat –
while the poor child's napping. That all you got?
I get sixteen years on and off with him
before someone else gets him. By *gets him*
you know what I mean. Here's a good one
of his birthmark and this might save you
time – his profile.

CODA

Don't ask how
everything worked out. Do you believe it?
Dre married his babymother, got a job
in Mississauga.

What did you expect?

I MEAN I

Recalculating, Recalculating

She's in her sixties, the churchlady in the passenger seat
who's all but saying we're lost because I'm driving
too fast. She leans forward and looks up *In 50 metres, turn right*
as if checking the weather. You should listen to the GPS man,
she says *Turn right* and dropping her voice,
He sounds irritated.
                        He's fine. We're fine. This is a shortcut.

                        Two minutes of forest and dotted line
later, she asks about my mother, what does she do?
only to gauge whether I plan to take her home or kill her,
dump the body over the guardrail. She sits on her hands.
I turn up the heat. *Recalculating.*
Recalculating.

                        She checks the sky again. I explain
that there is no British man in outer space wearing a headset
and tracking our movements along Route 117. Well, of course
there's no man in space, she says. It's all done via satellite.
He's probably in Delhi.
                        There's no man period, I say.
She corrects me. I correct her. Whose voice is that then?
It's nobody's voice. It's a man's voice. There is no one there
is someone there is no one there is someone there

Buffering, a sonnet

The video qua lity is poor. So's the sound.
The girl's mouth moves two seconds too late
to keep up with her voice. A cityscape
of cosmetics, perfume, and hairspray surrounds
her. For a moon, a gold doorknob in the background.
For three minutes seventeen seconds straight
she will rant on and on on how much she hates
excess body glitter. But somewhere around
minute two the stream freezes *buffering*,
buffering freezes her eyes as they sink,
her shocked mouth about to close on a word,
and when it seems that she will be fenced in
the webcam's silent field forever mouth open toward
the devourer, her voice finds her and she blinks.

Rapunzel

I'm letting down my long hair
you don't have to save me

just stay

I moved from the tower to an apartment
building. No stairs for you to climb, no scaling
up the sides. There's an elevator waiting.

Since the fiasco you've probably changed
your clothes, cut your hair or lost most of it,
but I'll know you still from the trail

of dotted lines you leave behind – tread marks
in snow, guidelines for scissors. I'll know you
from the swagger, from the horns heralding

your coming, from the hasty withdrawal.
The elevator will bell, its lips will open,
you will finger its buttons until it eats you.

Sweet talker, you will come back too
late to be of any use. Your girl's been caught,
disgraced, hair shorn before the twins

were born. Don't expect too much. Really
there's nothing (for you) to do up here (save me),
no music save (*me me me*) the twins crying.

If you don't come soon I'll consider jumping.

Which part did you love the best
me or the story : my hair or my hair

cut

THE COMMUTE

Nobody ever survives.

– Margaret Atwood

Ikemefuna certainly didn't
make it through the forest, pot of palm wine on his head,

with an entourage of slammer-mouthed men who led
him to believe he was going home. A lie, but they meant

well. Machete to the neck. Then the unnecessary announcement
My father they have killed me, present perfect, as if he were already dead.

And good weather, maps, company, trusty ship, work permits
didn't get all the Africans across, packed – like the Escher print

of birds morphing to fish – so you can't tell what you're seeing,
lost property, stolen goods. Even if they survived they didn't survive

to talk about it. And the driver of the tinted-windowed, chrome-
rimmed, black SUV who chose to eat a bagel in the traffic and not ride

the shoulder was still pulled over. No seatbelt. A small thing
relatively speaking. Easy to fix. Don't go out. Don't go home.

Returning home

            The good knife has aged.
It bites down weakly on an onion.

                My mother's gone
back to buying food we boys stretched faces at,
food she gave up praying over then lying about:
Brunswick sardines in mustard sauce, Digestives,
Cream of Wheat, high fibre/low fun cereals
with only French on the other side of the box.

Otherwise, no surprises. Don't mess with the stereo
presets, hands off the crystals, the airport souvenirs,
save half an onion or tomato or lemon for tomorrow,
open blinds in the morning, don't forget
them at night. Lock the front door. Make sure.

And leave the old gummy knife to chomp (my mother
waves my hand away). She does not see herself
on tiptoe, pressing down on it. *It's not dangerous* she says,
examining its smile. *It cuts perfectly.* Not well.

                Which means
she wasn't, as we thought all along, cooking up inconveniences
for us, but for herself.

            Else she doesn't care.
            Else she doesn't care
            anymore.

BUILD A V-SHAPED TORSO

You go understan or you go forget. If you cyah understan then
something wrong.

This is every boy's body's story.
13/14, the year of the separation when half his face
is no longer his, he looks at the dabs of white cream
under his ears, the fuzz in the sink, the blood on the razor
and thinks *ho ho I almost have a goatee* and tilts his chin
this way and that.

This is mine. I didn't know who I was
watching, whose face I was peeling mine to find: the white man
on the Yonge-University line shaking the finance section,
or the man with a girl in his armpit, nearly a headlock;
the man from "Those Winter Sundays" or from *Men's Health*
Build a V-Shaped Torso, Never Nick Yourself Again.
Didn't know until– yes, there should be an *until* here.

13/14, the year of the separation, my father said, *Boy*
when you older you go understan. Was that a promise
or a bet?

PASSAGE

                One spoon sometimes has to do
just suck it clean between the eggs and the oatmeal,
for dinner cornflake crumbs, that is if you want to eat
at all, the undershirt can go another day or two,

there's the radio for car music despite the static through
towns, brakes that whine but for the most part work, at least
till now, windshield for widescreen, backseat for loveseat,
remember for repeat. For the truth memory will do, will have to –

crust of a melody, a burnt kiss, some cheek in your hand
but all that's done. Sometimes one spoon has to do
the work of a knife, and student essays will have to sleep
with you, and if you're lucky get fresh about curfew, and
you better get used to used clothes, used mirrors too,
used mattresses, specially used words, whatever's cheap.

Passenger drop off

When our mother's last heeled foot stepped into the taxi
my brother pushed his arm through the wrought iron gate

of the Anglican school and said, just to be sure, *Mummy don't leave
me you know* and tracked the exhaust pipe to the vanishing point

as one might a plane taking off – which he did, come to think of it,
when she took off for a month to Brooklyn. He pretended not to know

her the night she returned sprinkling kisses, with sleepy spite he called
Mummy *Auntie* and Auntie *Mummy*.

                             Don't worry so much
about losing touch. You both root around your breast pockets

for each other: you have her business and she keeps your business
card in a kitchen drawer. At least she knows exactly where it is

and exactly who you are. And if you don't believe that, look
at the architecture of your hand, gloved in hers, the lines

on the palm nearly protractor perfect. Move your hand
to your wet eye or your keyboard and you move hers to hers.

O little bird, *ne t'inquiète pas*, open beaked at the edge of the V,
beating your wings *don't leave me, don't leave me.*

What remains of us

You said.
                You didn't hear what I said.

Everyone has left us.
I am the last one pulling
at the cord of her love.

We are all we
have. We are all
that remains of us,

that remains of some
past triumph, pressed
under the plastic shield
of photo albums.

                He didn't hear what I said.
                He wishes me dead for scalding him
                in the kitchen to unburn the fish.

                It's not about fish, son. It's about un.
                Listen: we're both angry
                at the wrong ones.

From him I've learned
to spit love out, to choke it,
one hand around my own neck.

An achievement: no man can
make her cry. Or so she says.
Smoke in the eyes, she explains
away everything. She explains
everything her way.

Sure, blame me for the fish
(we are all we have after all)
gutted, burnt, flaked black.
As she snaps at me, I snap
the fish spine with a fork.

I rot waiting
for him to say something,
the smallest dose of his laugh
will make me young again.

So long since his little fingers giggled
on my cheek, since the plumb weight
of his sausage legs and frilly socks
frolicked on my lap.

In the bindle of my jowls
I carry hard words
he doesn't want to hear.
There are things about you I know
and do not say.
True things. Misshapen.
There are things about you I know

and do not say *We are all we have.*
We have been reduced
to this. No cruelty.

Fry the fish.

I didn't say all the fish.
You said fry the fish.
I didn't mean all the fish.
You said fry the fish.
Not *all* the fish.
You said fry the fish.
Don't say *I said.* You *heard.*
You said.
You didn't hear what I said.
You said fry the fish.

When he was too young I made him
make his own lunch and it came back
home in shame: a croissant overwrapped
in plastic, crushed in the pocket of his bag.

My son, my boy, you are trying your best
and failing   but trying your best
and failing   but trying your best
(and failing) anyway.

Bruise.   Bruise.
Where is the man in the album?

Where else is he I mean
but in the album? Can she spot him

through the camouflage of memory,
without his fatigues, without the intent

to ambush? In the drowsy night
why does she start *who*? *who*?

at the doorbell or the telephone?
No one is coming back to us.

I am the only one at the end
of her love. We are all we have.

GONE

gone 1

g o
o n
o n e
e

gone 2

better places
perhaps elsewhere

better spaces
perhaps nowhere

gone 3

awaiting order
a knife bridge over jam

a cup's half smile
on the steel kettle

the room's spread
uncut by any body

gone 4

better or for worse
or just for good

ÉTUDE IN E, OP. 10, NO. 3

– Frédéric Chopin, bar 46

The phone interrupts a dark scale, a late
   night glissando down the black keys
      because I happen to be passing

by. The call is quick and quiet.
   I barely knew her, this woman
      no one really knew after 5:00.

Then, although it's late, I go outside and water
   the new mulberry and the grass seeds
      trying to sprout. *Lord she wasn't even 30.*

No one knew how long she was dead
   walking around the terminal
      of some disease waiting for her plane.

Had I been around instead of – Had I
   been around, I'd like to think, I would have known
      from her chipped French manicure,

from her mismatched purse and shoes,
   that death was strapped to her chest.
      Had I been around, were my hands not full

of *tristesse*, not practising the same wrecked bar
 of Chopin, the bar where the whole étude crashes
  into accidentals, the reckless intervals,

the hell-with-it bar where *Tristesse* jangles,
 I would have *what?* known *what?*
  enough *to what? to what? to watch?*

Must see

All Gaudi / 이 몸이 / how much fluke /so much
blahblahblah / so THIS THURSDAY AT 8/7 CENTRAL /
helix to heaven / the blow of Babel / backhand
through LEGO /
                 lipglossed backpacker
bejeweled /BROUGHT TO YOU BY/ curly headed
low into the collar, says *coquette*, says *forgive me my English* /
MEGA TELEVISION EVENT OF / spams love
in six tongues /이 몸이 / says *I show you La Sagrada Familia* /
crusting in ornament /so high its spires jook the sun /
DON'T MISS THE 2 HOUR FINALE / that we've seen it
and now /이 몸이 죽고 죽어 / ONLY ON /
一百番 고쳐 죽어 / kingdom come

COMEBACK

Surely I come quickly.
— Last recorded words

See? I'm talking like I know.
It's dangerous talking for Jesus.
You get carried away almost immediately.
— Naomi Shihab Nye

International terminal, arrivals section.
That's him. Tanned, sunglasses on his head,
a small tote bag like a leashed cocker spaniel
at his heels.

You shout *Jesus* and hold up your sign.
His eyes focus, his arms open to greet you.
Then you see it.

You?
I mean I.

Wrong floor. Maybe departures is where
all this happens. No one's rejoicing
to see him go

                  with his pilot uniform and cap
shepherding five virgin stewardesses
through the gate.

The other five are at the wrong counter
thinking they want to go to the Bahamas.
Paradise Island.

They?
Who knows? We?

Plane takes off.
Airport is lost
under clouds

of smoke.

It doesn't have to end like that.
He's not in the airport at all
or circling the sky for that matter.

He's driving loops around the terminal
refusing to spend the money to park.

He's expecting to see you
and your black childhood baggage
outside. The flight's delayed

as usual and security's coming
to scream a flashlight up in his face.

Two verses scroll across the LED board:

BOSTON	[16]heavenarchangel	SEOUL	trump	[17]caughtup	TORONTO	cloudsever
ONTIME	DELAYED	ARRIVED	DELAYED	ONTIME	ARRIVED	ONTIME

But you know that version.

You?
No, you.

Now's the wrong time

                                        to give up.
If you were going to you should have
given up a long time ago.

In the cane field or the Colosseum,
after the car accident, the divorce.
All those chances blown.

Next time. There'll be others. Next time
you're black or misbelieving, hound-hunted, kissed
on the cheek, jumped for your rings, cosigning
a car loan, wired shut at the jaw, locked
in the bathroom with the kids dialing the cops,
in a halo brace, hoisting a coffin on your shoulder,
jerking your elbow in the sunken mattress for some body
you now remember you've forgotten. Then.

On some overpasses in the deep banjo south
there are signs spraypainted in what could be blood: Not now
God ♡ *U. Jesus is coming. Repent. John 3:16.*

Might not mean much now that you're not   It's the wrong time
but driving on the unlit highway, choking in fog,
when the truck you were following for light   Too late
speeds off, and everyone in the car is asleep
save you   Not now
you believe
                                                                              It's the wrong time

the red spraypaint shining wet
in two rings of carlight.

                                                                              Wait

Acknowledgements

I am grateful to the Kimmel Harding Nelson Center for the Arts for a residency that enabled the completion of this manuscript. Special thanks also to the Cave Canem Foundation.

Thanks to the editors of the following publications in which these poems first appeared, sometimes in different forms and under different titles: *The Antigonish Review*: "Misunderstandings"; *Caduceus*: "Code White: Medical Emergency (Pediatric)" and "Code Red: Fire"; *Callaloo*: earlier versions of Emergency Codes; *Carousel*: "The Commute"; *Contemporary Verse 2*: "Special"; *The Drunken Boat*: "Open" and "The Commute"; *filling Station*: "Must see," "V"; *FSC Review*: "Mistakes"; *Gargoyle*: "West of Boston"; *Hacksaw*: "Étude in E, op. 10, no. 3"; *Margie*: "Rapunzel"; *Matrix*: "V"; *The Nashwaak Review*: "Not saying," "Notwithstanding" and "Not answering"; *Pebble Lake Review*: "What remains of us" and "Returning home"; *PLUMb*: "Comeback"; *Timber Creek Review*: "Build a V-Shaped Torso"; "V" appeared electronically as Leaf Press's Monday poem.

The Alice Munro epigraph to this collection comes from the title story of *Who Do You Think You Are?* (Toronto: Macmillan, 1978). The Judith Butler epigraph is from the second chapter of *Precarious Life: The Powers of Mourning and Violence* (New York: Verso, 2004). In the poem, "Except you," Speyside is a town in Tobago. The epigraph to "The Commute" is from Margaret Atwood's "Roominghouse, winter"; Ikemefuna is a character from Chinua Achebe's *Things Fall Apart*. In "Must see," the text, 이 몸이 죽고 죽어 一百番 고쳐 죽어, is from a traditional Korean poem (Sijo) by Jung Mong Ju. It can be translated, "My body may die again and again, one hundred times again." Epigraphs to "Comeback" are from Revelation 22:20 and Naomi Shihab Nye's "I feel sorry for Jesus." At the end of the poem, the verses in superscript are truncations of 1 Thessalonians 4:16–17.

I'd like to thank a small assembly line of people who helped shape this book: Jim Johnstone, my first reader, with whom I swapped poems on northbound trains; Rhea Tregebov, rare ambidextrous poet/editor, who knows just what to say to a poem to make its heart palpitate; Joseph Yau, yes, in the dedication; my shift of 3:30 writers: Kaitlin Hanger, Ben Stein, Suzanne Owens, George Mahoney, Marcy Colalillo, Patrick Cuff, Matthew Raymond; colleagues at Fitchburg State College, particularly Ben Railton, Leon Weinmann, Eve Rifkah, Bornali Bhandari, Sean Goodlett and Clair Degutis for reading and listening; Peter Lucic and Ursula Keuper-Bennett for childhood's pre-production; Irina Souiki for the cover photograph of cubes, taken, appropriately enough, inside Terminal 1 of Toronto's Pearson Airport; designer Jared Roberts, who makes viewing as pleasurable as eating; and Noelle Allen, Lindsay Hodder and the Wolsak and Wynn team, champions of Canadian poetry. Finally, I wish to thank my family, my mother, Judy Williams, especially, who better than anyone understands the wordless after-hours factory and the damage.